John Peter Zenger

Free Press Advocate

Karen T. Westermann

Arthur M. Schlesinger, jr.
Senior Consulting Editor

Chelsea House Publishers

Philadelphia

Produced by Pre-Press Company, Inc., East Bridgewater, MA 02333

CHELSEA HOUSE PUBLISHERS
Editor in Chief Stephen Reginald
Production Manager Pamela Loos
Art Director Sara Davis
Director of Photography Judy L. Hasday
Managing Editor James D. Gallagher
Senior Production Editor J. Christopher Higgins

Staff for JOHN PETER ZENGER
Project Editor Anne Hill
Associate Art Director Takeshi Takahashi
Series Design Keith Trego

The Chelsea House World Wide Web address is http://www.chelseahouse.com

First Printing
1 3 5 7 9 8 6 4 2

Library of Congress Cataloging-in-Publication Data

Westermann, Karen T.
    John Peter Zenger / Karen T. Westermann.
        p. cm. — (Colonial leaders)
    Includes bibliographical references (p.) and index.
    ISBN 0-7910-5966-9 (HC); 0-7910-6123-X (PB)
        1. Zenger, John Peter, 1697–1746—Juvenile literature. 2. Printers—
    United States—Biography—Juvenile literature. 3. Freedom of the press—
    United States—History—18th century—Juvenile literature 4. Zenger,
    John Peter, 1697–1746—Trials, litigation, etc.—Juvenile literature.
        5. Trials (Seditious libel)—New York (State)—Juvenile literature. 6. Printing—
    New York (State)—History—18th century—Juvenile literature. [1. Zenger,
    John Peter, 1697–1746. 2. Printers. 3. Freedom of the press.] I. Title. II. Series.

Z232.Z5 W47 2000
686.2'092—dc21
[B]   00-038401

Contents

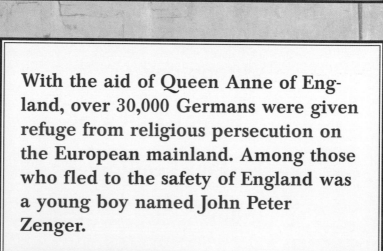

With the aid of Queen Anne of England, over 30,000 Germans were given refuge from religious persecution on the European mainland. Among those who fled to the safety of England was a young boy named John Peter Zenger.

Fighting to Be Free

When John Peter Zenger was born in 1697, his mother and father were hiding in the mountains of the Black Forest in western Germany. They lived in hiding because it was a time of war between the Germans and the French.

A few years later, they again had to run away. This time, both French and German soldiers wanted to kill them. It was not because they had done anything bad. It was because of their religion—how they chose to pray to God. They went to a country that was next to theirs called the Netherlands, also known as Holland. For five years, Peter's family and thousands of other people from the Lower Palatinate on the Rhine River in Germany worked on farms in the Netherlands.

Then, once more, the Zenger family was not safe. With the other Germans, or Palatines, as they were called, they had to run away. King Louis XIV of France was a mean ruler, a tyrant, who burned their houses and farm crops. Families were starving when Queen Anne of England saved them. She sent a fleet of ships to a river city in the Netherlands, called Rotterdam, to bring the 30,000 **refugees** to her country.

Like many, the Zengers hoped they would be able to make a home for themselves in England. They wanted a warm place to sleep and cook and eat. They wanted a place to laugh and play. They needed jobs to do this but there was not enough work to be found. After two years of struggling, the **British** government offered many families free passage to America. They also promised to lend them money. In return for sending them to America, England wanted the

Many people considered King Louis XIV of France a tyrant. His dislike of the Palatines resulted in the burning of their homes and crops. Many Palatines suffered from starvation as a result before finally fleeing to England.

The German immigrants who came to America's colonies were said to be the best farmers, the hardest workers, and the least wasteful. When they cut trees for their log cabin homes, they used any left-over wood for fencing, rails, and firewood. They did without extras and fancy things so they could save their money.

people to tap the pine forests to make tar and turpentine for English ships.

Peter was 13 years old now. (Even though his full name was John Peter Zenger, he was called Peter and usually signed his name J. Peter Zenger.) He had spent his whole life longing to be free. Along with his father, mother, younger brother, and sister, he set sail on a wooden ship with almost 300 other Germans. They sailed across the Atlantic Ocean for 75 days. Their ship was overcrowded and there was not enough food or water for all of them. Thirty people died of fevers. Sadly, Peter's father was one of them.

When they finally arrived in New York on a hot summer day in 1710, what they saw was a small town with red brick houses and blue roofs.

Right in front of them was a long, old, gray fort. Next to the fort were the gallows for hanging people who had been sentenced to die for a crime. There were some warehouses and above those were the church steeples.

A city official welcomed the newcomers. At the time of Zenger's arrival, Peter could see that New York was small compared to the old cities in Europe. It did not take long to walk through the streets to an open field called the Common. In the Common, there were rows of white tents for the refugees to stay in. They were not the first ones to arrive though. Other tents were filled with 3,000 other Palatines who had sailed to America earlier. Four hundred of them had died of fever, too. Peter and the other refugees were in a faraway place where everything was new and different. They were glad to find friends from back home.

Wandering up and down the streets, the new-comers could find tradesmen: a cobbler who made shoes; a blacksmith who made things of

In the 1700s and early 1800s, most boys finished their schooling at 12 or 14 and became apprenticed to a master craftsman. Apprentices were boys who worked beside the blacksmith, carpenter, weaver, or printer for long hours. They did not get paid, but they learned the trade by helping the master. Often, a contract was signed, and the boy lived with the tradesman's family. He had to follow the family's rules and do chores.

metal, such as horseshoes, latches, hinges, and farm tools; a tailor who made clothes; and a printer who printed pamphlets and newspapers.

Most tradesmen had apprentices. Peter became interested in becoming a printer's apprentice. The apprentice worked on a big wooden machine called a printing press. It was like a table with heavy wooden braces at each side that held up a huge wooden screw that was six inches thick. The screw stood straight up in the middle. The apprentice turned the screw and raised a flat piece that was attached to the bottom. He pulled out a piece of paper from between the flat piece and the table, put in another piece of paper and pressed down the lid once more. He

Print shops were one of the many colonial businesses that offered apprenticeships to young boys. It was as a printer's apprentice that John Peter Zenger first developed his interest in one day owning a press of his own.

did this by pushing a long handle that was stuck in the top end of the screw. Pulling on the handle was very hard to do, and it took much strength.

Many printers had to make their own paper. Linen rags were washed, cut into pieces, and boiled with lye in a large kettle. The rags were then shredded in a machine called a hollander. The watery pulp was placed in a large container called a vat and then scooped into a paper-making mold. The water was drained and the thin layer of pulp was dropped onto a felt pad. This layer was then placed beneath a press, and the water was carefully squeezed out. The sheets were laid out to dry to become paper.

When Peter first asked the master printer in New York if he could be an apprentice too, the printer wanted to know who would pay his apprentice fee. Since Peter's father had died on the ship and his family needed all of their money for food, the printer was not able to help Peter.

What was he going to do? Like others boys with no money, he could have sold himself as a servant who would chop wood, carry water, dig ditches and graves, or drive a cart. He would probably have had rags for clothes and would have earned very little money.

Life was hard indeed and people were sick everywhere. The citizens of New York were worried because the fever that had killed so many of the Palatines was spreading. Men, women, and children were dying. It was decided that these newcomers would go to Nutten Island. (Later, the name would be changed to Governor's Island.) Governor Hunter reported what was going on in a letter he sent to London, England:

> The poor Palatines have been mighty sickly but are rapidly recovering. We have lost over 470 of our number. I have been obliged to purchase 6,000 acres for them on Hudson's River about 100 miles up, where they are to be planted in five villages on both sides of the river. I am making all possible haste to send them before the winter.

The Palatines were on the move again. This time, the governor told them that they could have a plot of land in the villages on the Hudson River. They had to promise they would build a house, clear a field, and plant crops. They also had to make a certain amount of tar or turpentine from the trees. They were given two years to pay all taxes and fees. The agreement also stated that children eight years and older would help the adults.

Peter was too young to be given land but, after waiting a long time to go to one of the villages, his luck changed. He got to leave Nutten Island and go to one of the villages on the Hudson River. He also got his wish; he was going to be an apprentice to a printer, and his brother was going to be an apprentice to a carpenter. The government paid for their apprenticeships. Mrs. Zenger got a job in a big house as a nurse to a large family. Most of her work was sewing clothes for the children and Peter's little sister stayed with her.

Peter lived with the printer, William Bradford, and his family. He ate with them, prayed with them, and when he misbehaved, he got a spanking. But the Bradfords also treated him kindly. Peter worked six days a week and on

Along the banks of the Hudson River, a number of small villages were created for use by the Palatines. It was in one such village that John Peter Zenger received his first apprenticeship in the shop of printer William Bradford.

Sundays, he and his brother got to visit their mother and sister.

How did Peter have time for school? The law said that the master tradesmen had to teach their students how to read, write, and do arithmetic. Sometimes Bradford taught Peter himself, but

An apprenticeship to a printer usually lasted for seven years. The first year was usually very hard because the apprentice had to do work from morning until night and do many chores. After the first year, he started learning the "art and mastery" of printing. He was given a handwritten article that he had to "set in type" one letter at a time. He had to get each letter from a big wooden case of drawers and put them into a slotted stick. He then had to set all the letters backward so they would come out the right way once they were printed. This is how books and newspapers were printed.

when he was too busy, Peter went to Andrew Clarke's Grammar Free School. He had to go in the evenings, though, because Bradford wanted Peter to do as much work as possible.

Peter spent eight years, from 1710 to 1718, as an apprentice to Bradford. At the end of that time, when he was 21 years old, he decided to move to another state. He went to Maryland and opened up his own shop. He got married, and a son was born in 1719, but his wife died when his son was still an infant. When he was 24, he went back to William Bradford in New York and asked for a job. Mr. Bradford hired him as a **journeyman.**

There were big changes in store for Peter. Three months later, Peter married again. His wife's name was Anna Catharina Maulin (Catherine, as she would be called). She was a poor Dutch girl, however, she was smart and a hard worker. With his wife by his side, Peter's dream of becoming a printer came true.

With the arrival of the *Seaford* in New York's harbor, several events occurred that shaped the course of American history. The cause of these events was the introduction of a new governor to the colony—the corrupt William Cosby. Facing off against Cosby, Zenger began his fight to establish a free press.

2

The Newspaper Business

Before the American Revolution in 1775 and the Treaty of Paris that ended the war in 1783, the American colonies were under British rule. The king of England chose men to be governors in the American colonies. These governors had the most power because they were carrying out the laws of England and the wishes of the king. At the same time, the well-being of the citizens depended on the governors' policies and how he governed them.

William Cosby arrived in New York on August 1, 1732, on the king's ship, the *Seaford*. It was not long after he came that some people in New York were hearing stories about Governor Cosby which were not good. Before Cosby had come to New York, he had been sent by the English government to be the governor in Minorca, Spain. While in Minorca, he spent government money on himself. Also, after an argument with a Spanish merchant, he took tobacco from him and sold it for a lot of money. All of this made the people of Minorca so angry that they had him sent back to England. To make matters worse, on his way back home, Cosby spent all of the money on his travels across Europe.

Once back in England, he was tried and found guilty of taking the government's money in Minorca. How did such a man end up as governor of New York? Once he was found guilty at his trial, he either had to pay the money back or go to jail. Lucky for him, he had friends who loaned him the 10,000 **pounds** he needed, but they wanted to be repaid. These friends were powerful people and they arranged to have him appointed governor of New York and New Jersey. The men knew that as a governor he could earn the money to pay them back.

The former governor of New York had died and the oldest member of the local governing body, His Majesty's Council, 72-year-old Rip Van Dam, was a temporary governor for 13 months. The job was not an easy one but it paid well. The people of New York liked Van Dam. One of the reasons they liked him was that he did not try to take advantage of taxpayers to make himself rich like many governors did.

When Cosby arrived with his wife, two older sons, and two teenage daughters, a welcoming committee met the family's ship at the waterfront. When Cosby met Van Dam, he wanted to know how much he would be paid for the time before he came to New York. Van Dam told him that his salary began now, since he had only just arrived. Cosby argued that he had done work in England in preparation for his job and he expected to be paid. Cosby's attitude shocked the welcoming committee.

Things only got worse. One of the first things he did as governor was to buy new uniforms and equipment for the American soldiers. He paid for them at British prices and charged the government American prices. The tricky part was that the American prices were twice the British prices, so he made a lot of money and kept it for himself. He also collected money he said was for the Indians and never gave it to them. Cosby also refused to give some settlers land unless he could keep one third of it for himself.

There were many examples of his greed, and trouble was brewing in New York because of it. Peter Zenger was just one of the people who was listening to the talk about the governor. Cosby convinced the New York **legislature** to give him money for work he said he did for them even before he left England. They offered him 750 pounds but he violently objected and demanded more. He got 1,000 pounds more and kept up this behavior until he got another 8,000 pounds. Still this was not enough to pay

King George II ordered that William Cosby and Rip Van Dam were to share the money both had made after Cosby's appointment as governor of New York. A pamphlet printed by Zenger made it impossible for Cosby to seek more money than he had earned, which greatly upset Cosby.

back the friends in England who had saved him from jail.

He tried something else, but it proved to be a mistake. He wanted the king of England to give him half of the salary Van Dam earned as acting governor. But Van Dam was clever and not about to hand over more money to Cosby. The king had ordered that Cosby and Van Dam share equally the money that both of them had earned before Cosby came to New York. Cosby asked for half of Van Dam's salary– 900 pounds. Van Dam, however, had a friend in London who did some detective work for him. He found out that according to the king's order, Cosby owed Van Dam more than 3,500 pounds. Peter Zenger printed this information in a pamphlet and made it impossible for Cosby to take any more money from Van Dam.

Peter grew restless working for William Bradford. A newspaper's purpose is to print the news of the day. The fact was that Bradford was paid by the government. His title was printer to the king, and it was the king of England who had sent the new governor to New York. If Bradford made Governor Cosby angry, he would lose his job. He also feared he would go to jail if he printed anything that displeased Cosby. As a younger man in Philadelphia, he had come close to going to jail for printing articles against the government. He did not want to risk that again, especially at his age. Because of his concerns, Bradford's newspaper, the *Gazette,* was not very interesting.

Peter was not the only one who thought this. As it turned out, two wealthy and important men were angry at what Governor Cosby was doing and they wanted to do something about it. Lewis Morris Jr., son of Chief Justice of New York, Lewis Morris, and James Alexander, New York's finest lawyer, discovered that Peter thought as they did. They asked him if he would print their articles about Cosby. Peter explained that he would print their articles if he had his own shop. When the two gentlemen found out that Peter did not have all of the money to buy his own equipment, they offered to help him pay to start his own business.

Once in his new shop, Peter printed a 36-page, unsigned pamphlet for Lewis Morris Jr. that talked about the problems with the government. Hundreds of copies were sold and all of New York was talking about the article. This was the chance Peter had hoped for–to print what he pleased, to stand up to people who were not fair and just. But Peter had to make enough money to support his wife and children, too. He could not do this just by selling articles. He also needed to print books. At first Peter did well and he was so busy that his wife, Catherine, had to help him. She learned how to set type, sew the pages, bind the books, and manage the shop.

Things did not continue to go well for the Zengers. Peter was slow at his work, his spelling was not good, and his bindings were not neat. Most people stopped bringing their work to him. He took a job as a church organist but it did not pay much.

During this time, something happened that caught Peter's attention. One day while he was reading the *Pennsylvania Gazette,* a newspaper from Philadelphia, he noticed that a new publisher had bought it—Benjamin Franklin. He was the same person who had been writing the *Busy Body Papers,* a series that had people talking. So when Peter saw that Franklin was also printing a paper, he read it closely. He showed it to Catherine too. The articles were exciting; they talked about disagreements in government matters. It was bold and, best of all, people wanted to read it. Peter and Catherine decided to sell it in their printing shop.

John Peter Zenger opened a print shop, much like the one seen here, and began printing articles and pamphlets which attacked corruption in the colony of New York.

Benjamin Franklin was a great influence on the life of John Peter Zenger. Zenger sold Franklin's very successful *Busy Body Papers* in his shop. Also, it was the influence of Franklin's newspaper, the *Pennsylvania Gazette,* which would help the Zengers develop their own interest in starting a paper.

While Peter was interested in publishing a newspaper of his own, not just articles now and then and a few books, he did not have the money. In the meantime, he and Catherine thought it would be a good idea to study Ben Franklin's paper to see what made it so popular.

This turned out to be a good idea. Before too long, Zenger would have a chance to publish his own newspaper. Governor Cosby was not about to give up fighting for what he wanted, no matter what he had to do to get it. In the end, it was Governor Cosby's actions that led to the start of Zenger's own newspaper.

In early colonial days only men of property were considered eligible to vote or serve on a jury. In New York, such men were sympathetic with a fellow property owner like Van Dam, and this did not help Cosby's cause.

The Power of the Press

William Cosby was determined to take the 900 pounds from Rip Van Dam. When Van Dam refused, Cosby decided to try him in court, but he knew that a New York jury would not force Van Dam to pay him. So, he formed a new court to try him—one that had no jury. This so alarmed Van Dam, Alexander, Morris, and others that they had a meeting to discuss what was going on.

Cosby's new court would be made up of the judges who sat in the Supreme Court, but Chief Justice Lewis Morris Sr. was not asked about it. When he got word of what was happening, he was very angry.

He said that the governor had no right to go against the wishes of the assembly that the people had elected. Not long after this, Cosby removed Lewis Morris Sr. as chief justice.

Governor Cosby also took it upon himself to expel Lewis Morris Jr. from His Majesty's Council because Morris had criticized him. (But then Morris was elected to the legislative assembly.) Things were really heating up and there was no mention of anything in William Bradford's *Gazette* since he worked for the king and could not say anything against the king's appointed governor.

Lewis Morris Jr. and James Alexander were the leaders who were forming a new political party—the Popular Party. They wanted Governor Cosby sent back to England or they wanted to force him to behave in a fair manner. They needed a weekly newspaper with a publisher who would help them fight their battle. They asked Peter Zenger if he would be their printer. He wanted to, but Peter did not have enough money to publish a weekly paper. Lewis Morris agreed to cover the costs of running the newspaper. Another problem was that Zenger had little education and experience. It was decided that James Alexander would be the editor.

Still, Zenger worried about what would happen if he printed articles that angered the governor. Cosby did, after all, have power over the judges. Would Zenger go to jail? William Bradford had hinted to Peter about a time when he had been threatened with jail when he was a young printer in Pennsylvania. And Bradford's son had

William Bradford was born in England and served as an apprentice to a printer in London. After moving to Philadelphia, he set up his first print shop and then his own paper mill. During his time in Philadelphia, William Bradford published a pamphlet which was critical of the Quakers. He was arrested on charges of being libelous to the Quakers, who were very influential in Pennsylvania. Bradford was brought to trial and found innocent. The result of the trial was one of the colonies' first victories in establishing freedom of the press. Bradford would later move to New York, where he opened another print shop and began publishing the *Gazette*—New York's first newspaper.

At a very young age, Benjamin Franklin was apprenticed in the print shop of his brother, James, who published the *New England Courant*. While an apprentice, Franklin secretly contributed articles to his brother's paper. In 1723 he moved to Philadelphia, where he began his own press. He would go on to publish the *Pennsylvania Gazette, Poor Richard's Almanac,* and the *Busy Body Papers*. He is sometimes called the "wisest American," having played an important role in early American diplomacy and the drafting of the U.S. Constitution.

been jailed for a short time in Pennsylvania for printing Benjamin Franklin's *Busy Body Papers*.

A chance came for the new Popular Party to test just how popular it was. An **assemblyman** (a member of the local government) in Westchester County died and, as governor, Cosby had to call a special election so the citizens could vote for a new assemblyman. Judge Morris, whom Cosby had expelled from the Supreme Court, was going to run as a candidate for this position. During the election, the sheriff, who was appointed by Cosby, said the religious group called Quakers could not vote because they would not take an oath that

Benjamin Franklin began his writing career when he secretly contributed articles to his brother's paper in Boston. He later created quite a stir when he first printed his *Busy Body Papers*.

they were landowners. It was against the Quakers' religion to swear to an oath; the law said they could make an affirmation (stating that something is as they say it is) instead. Thirty-eight Quakers wanted to vote for the Popular Party, but the sheriff refused to let them. Even

The Quakers became a thorn in Governor
Cosby's side when they attempted to vote
for the Popular Party. Despite Cosby's re-
fusal to let them vote due to their religious
beliefs, the Popular Party won the election.
One of the first stories to run in Zenger's
paper described the events surrounding
the election.

without their votes, Morris and the Popular Party won by a vote of 231 to 151, and many people celebrated. The victory encouraged the people to continue their fight against Governor Cosby.

The first *New York Weekly Journal* was printed on November 5, 1733. It had the story of the Westchester election, including the part about the Quakers. The first edition (copy) was sold out by 9 A.M. The Zengers printed another edition, then a third, to keep up with all of the people who wanted a copy. There were a few mistakes and misspellings, but still the paper sold.

Voting in the early colonial days was considered a privilege —a special right, not an automatic one. Only a few members in the community could vote: white men who owned property, either land or money, and went to church in the colony's official church. Women, Native Americans, free blacks, and slaves were not allowed to vote. Starting with U.S. independence, voting laws grew less strict. In 1865 the Fifteenth Amendment was passed that gave black men the right to vote, and in 1920, women were given the right to vote.

Governor Cosby decided to fight back using William Bradford's *Gazette.* He asked Judge Francis Harrison to edit the newspaper so he could respond to the *Journal.* Harrison wrote that the governor was good and honorable, but he did not say anything about Zenger. The *Journal* continued its articles. It did not name Governor Cosby but it said that "Some governors may certainly err, misbehave, and become criminal." It told how Governor Cosby had destroyed the deed to the Indians' land and had illegally gotten rid of the Supreme Court chief justice for refusing to take orders. Zenger himself wrote humorous articles that the Court Party did not think were funny. He wrote about them as animals. Mr. Alexander brought articles for Zenger to print that were not signed. If there was no author, no one could be arrested for writing them.

Of course, Governor Cosby was angry that he was being attacked. He realized that Peter could not be running the newspaper by himself. He knew Zenger was too poor, so he assumed that the person paying for it was Van Dam, who still refused to give Cosby half of his salary. Cosby had a plan. He had called Van Dam to court so many times that Van Dam finally stopped coming. Cosby thought he could say that Van Dam could not be found and that he was running from the law. If Cosby could present this to the court, he could take Van Dam's properties: houses, ships, a ship-building yard, and a new theater that he had opened. Cosby needed witnesses, so he arranged to have three sailors get drunk enough to sign papers saying that Van Dam was to be arrested. Cosby's plan did not work, however. When the sailors' captain heard about it, he was very upset. He had treated Governor Cosby well, but when he discovered the dishonest thing Cosby had done to Van Dam, one of the city's most honorable citizens, he made his men go to the city official to swear in writing that they had been tricked and the whole thing was a lie.

Still Cosby would not give up. This time, he formed a grand jury of 19 New York citizens. The men were chosen by the sheriff from the book of voters. The new chief justice was Judge James Delancey, assigned by Cosby. If the judge displeased the governor, he could be dismissed by him. The grand jury was told that there was a newspaper that was printing articles against the very governor the king of England had sent to govern them. It did not matter if the statements in the articles were true or not; whoever printed them would be accused of going against the government and of hurting a person's reputation.

Judge Delancey told the jurors they were to **indict** either Van Dam or Peter Zenger. The jurors took all day to make a decision and when they returned to the courtroom the next day, the only decision they had made was to have the judge's charges printed. In other words, they refused to indict either Van Dam or Zenger. Printed words had come up against a big power and won. Peter could continue printing his newspaper.

And continue he did. Van Dam was ready for battle. He brought in a 60-page pamphlet to be published and Zenger printed the following:

ADVERTISEMENT

There is now printing and will shortly be published and to be sold by the printer of this paper, *The Proceedings of Rip Van Dam, Esq., in order for obtaining equal justice of his Excellency William Cosby, Esq.,* by which it seemeth that said Van Dam believes an attack has been made in his province on the privilege of juries.

The pamphlet explained what had happened with the three drunken sailors. New Yorkers liked Van Dam and were angry at what Governor Cosby had done. They reasoned that if the governor could get around the law by using three drunken soldiers, then what good were the laws? They also thought that if an important man like Van Dam with two lawyers could be attacked, what chance did the common man have against such a government? Cosby had no choice but to drop the false charges against Van Dam. He knew that a governor in 1709 had gone to jail. He knew too that Van Dam had been one of the main leaders against another governor, Leisler, who was publicly hanged in 1691.

The battle was like a game of chess with both sides seeing how far they could go. Zenger's newspaper grew bolder, wanting to know why the citizens had to be governed by "a fellow only one degree better than an idiot," who cursed and had "nothing human but a shape."

Now, the *Gazette* was naming Zenger and his newspaper in their articles. Judge Harrison, who had been writing the *Gazette* articles, went a step further. He wrote an unsigned letter threatening the family of James Alexander, the *Journal's* editor. Zenger found witnesses who swore that the handwriting was Harrison's and printed the entire letter in his paper along with the sworn testimony of the witnesses. In this newspaper, he also challenged Governor Cosby's "special court" which had no jury. He outlined the reasons why such a court was illegal. The special court never tried one case.

After reporting many illegal actions by Cosby, the *Journal* went so far as to say that the governor should return to England.

After Governor Cosby had been in New York for two years, it was time for the people to elect their 14 **aldermen.** The people of New York were tired of the aldermen who represented them because they treated them unfairly. The election was held, and once again the Court Party cheated by sneaking in voters who did not live in the district. Judge Delancey allowed it, but when the votes were counted, the Popular Party still had more votes.

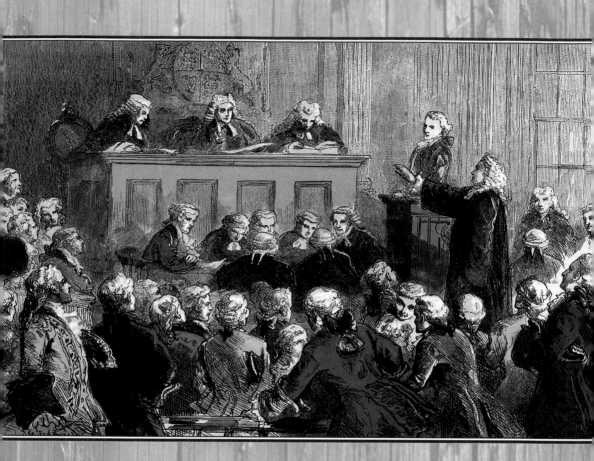

Governor Cosby's anger with John Peter
Zenger grew until eventually he had
Zenger arrested for *libel* and *sedition*–the
punishment for which would have been
death. The trial that followed proved to be
one of the defining moments in American
history.

Imprisonment

Attacks on both sides continued, and Governor Cosby took a bold step. If he could not indict Peter Zenger, then he would demand that the newspapers that had run articles against him be "burnt by the hands of the common hangman, or whipper, near the pillory in this city on Wednesday, the 6th instant, between the hours of eleven and twelve in the forenoon." The sheriff was sent to collect the papers from Zenger but the ones he needed were not there. In the end, some copies of the paper were found that could be burned, but the hangman did not show up and no one else would

In 1734, the city of New York had a population of about 10,000 inhabitants, of whom fully 1,700 were African slaves. On the west side of the island, above what is now Cortlandt Street, there was only an occasional house and the same was true of the east side north of Frankfort Street. The south end of the city was also much less developed than today. In 1731 there were only 1,500 houses in the city, and in the same year, it was recorded that quail could be killed in the brush east of what is now Broadway.

burn them. They ordered a slave to do it.

Cosby was trying to find out who the writers of the *Journal* were. This time he tried to bribe James Alexander's slave. Cosby sent word through a lawyer that he would give the slave enough money to buy him his freedom if he would listen at the Alexanders' parties and find out who was doing the writing for the *Journal*. But the slave would not be unfaithful; instead he told the *Journal* writers, Alexander and Morris, about the offer.

Cosby would not give up. This time he offered a 50-pound reward for anyone giving the names of the *Journal* writers and posting them in the taverns. If someone did tell and Zenger was

As the influence of Zenger's paper grew, a judge ordered that the existing copies of the paper be burned for everyone in the city to witness. The judge's wishes were put on hold, though, when the local hangman refused to take part in the burning.

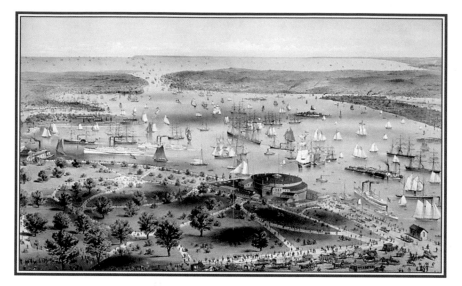

The New York City we know today is a far cry from the one in which Zenger lived. Where New York City now has a population of over 7 million people, in 1734 the population was close to 10,000.

found guilty, the punishment for sedition was having your ears chopped off, and the punishment for libel was hanging. When no one came forward to say who wrote the articles, Judge Delancey then made another offer to Peter; if he would tell who the writers were, Cosby would give him 100 pounds. Peter refused.

On November 17, 1734, John Peter Zenger was placed under arrest by an order from His Majesty's Council. Judge Harrison came with the sheriff to take him to jail. His cell was small, dark, cold, and damp. There were insects and rats. Straw covered the floor and there was a three-legged stool and a small table. He had to pay for his own dinner. They would not let his wife or a lawyer visit him, although most prisoners were usually allowed these rights.

The next morning, Alexander and William Smith, his law partner and friend, went to see him at the jail. They would be Zenger's lawyers. They told him that Lewis Morris Sr. was about to sail to England to ask the king for help. In the meantime, the lawyers would represent him and try to arrange **bail** for him. They explained how this trial was not only about one man printing against another, but it would be about all the people of America having freedom from governors who did not follow the very law they were supposed to uphold.

His lawyers argued that it was illegal for a prisoner not to be able to write or speak to anyone, so he was given pencil and paper, and his wife, Catherine, was allowed to see him. She assured him that with the help of their son and the journeyman, she would continue to publish the paper. Peter would write articles from his jail cell. Bail was set at 400 pounds, so high that he could not afford to pay it. Alexander wanted to raise money to pay it, but Zenger refused. He believed it was too much money for his friends to spend on him, so Peter stayed in jail.

Governor Cosby must have been surprised when new copies of the *Journal* appeared while Peter was in jail. Peter wrote letters from jail and there were also copies of documents from the court case against Peter. It was Catherine who kept the paper organized. She managed the money, bought ink and paper, set the type, proofread the pages, and wrote the news from Europe. She taught her children how to help.

Prisons during the 1700s were dark, dirty, and a haven for disease. After Zenger's arrest, he was locked away in one such prison.

Looking back at history, this was an important time of challenge against the government and an important time of change in the colonies. The stage was being set for new freedoms. One example involved Judge Francis Harrison, who

A grand jury is selected to inquire into crimes and determine if there is need for a criminal prosecution. It is called a grand jury because it tends to be larger than a jury used in a normal trial. A grand jury is assembled to hear evidence and only approves indictments (an order that someone brought to criminal trial) when it is satisfied that there is enough evidence gathered against the accused. In the 17th century the grand jury acquired its modern function; it prevents an unjustified or politically motivated prosecution from ever going to trial.

had been charged with committing several crimes but had not been tried. The new aldermen insisted on forming a new grand jury. The grand jury voted to indict Harrison. When the police went to arrest him, he was not there. He had run away, and his family never heard from him again.

In the meantime, Peter waited in jail. Finally, at the end of January, the sheriff told him that the grand jury had no charges against him. Peter would be free, or so he thought. The **attorney general** had a trick up his sleeve; he filed an information on Zenger. Alexander explained to Peter what that meant. When he had been attorney general, there was a law that said you could force anyone to stand trial for any reason. It was just as though there was a real charge against him by a grand jury. When Alexander had been attorney general, he never used an information, but then Bradley came into office and started using it again. In 1766, Lewis Morris Jr., as a member of His Majesty's Council, wrote a law against it and had it passed in the legislature. There was one way to get around the law. The law said that the attorney general could use an information if he got the chief justice of New York to sign it. When the law was written, Lewis Morris Sr. was the chief justice and no one thought there would be problems. But the judges now in office had been appointed by Cosby and the governor had control over them. If they behaved in a way that displeased the governor, he could let them go.

The information law meant that Zenger had to go back to jail for another three months. When he appeared in the courtroom in April, hundreds of people were packed inside. The first thing Zenger's lawyers, Alexander and Smith, did was ask for a new judge. They told Judge Delancey that he could not possibly give Zenger a fair trial because Governor Cosby would dismiss any judge who did not carry out his wishes. This brought a dramatic answer from Judge Delancey. He told them that they were disbarred, which meant that they could no longer practice law and, of course, could not be Zenger's lawyers. Alexander and Smith were outraged. Their life's work ended in one moment.

Zenger had no choice but to ask for a court-appointed lawyer and the only lawyers available were members of the Court Party or those who were afraid of Judge Delancey. John Chambers was Zenger's new lawyer. He had run for office during the elections as a Court Party candidate. He lost to the Popular Party. Did this mean that Peter would be defended by the "enemy"?

Things were not quite as dark as they seemed. For one thing, a lawyer had a duty to defend his client. Second, a lawyer wants to win cases, not lose them. Third, when Chambers lost the Court Party election, he realized how strong the Popular Party was and how many people did not like Governor Cosby. He also learned who some of the Popular Party supporters were–and how much land and influence they had.

The court date was set for August 4, 1735. While Peter was sitting in his jail cell, other people were working on his case. Former judge Morris was in London trying to convince the British government to call Governor Cosby back to England, but he was not having much luck.

Toward the end of July, it was time to select a **jury** for the trial. Zenger knew that since the judge already thought him guilty, his only chance to avoid being hanged was the jury. From an explanation of what happened, written by Zenger himself after the trial, he tells about the jury selection: "On Tuesday, July 29, 1735, the Court opened. On the motion of Mr. Chambers

[Zenger's lawyer] for a **struck jury,** . . . the Court were of the opinion that I was entitled to have a struck jury. That evening at five o'clock some of my friends attended the clerk for striking the jury; when to their surprise the clerk, instead of producing the Freeholders book, to strike the jury from it in their presence as usual, produced a list of 48 persons whom he said he had taken out of the Freeholders book." The selection of a fair jury was a problem that had to be solved before the trial could begin. Zenger continues: "My friends told him [the clerk] that a great number of these persons were not freeholders; that others were persons holding . . . offices at the Governor's pleasure; that others were . . . supposed to have resentment against me for what I had printed concerning them; that others were the Governor's baker, tailor, shoemaker, candlemaker, joiner, etc.; that as to the few indifferent men that were upon that list, they had reason to believe (as they had heard) that Mr. Attorney [Bradley] had a list of them, to strike them out. And therefore they requested that he would either bring the Freeholders book, and choose out of it 48 unexceptional men in their presence as usual." The clerk refused to do this, and Chambers had to speak to the court about it. "And the Court upon his motion ordered that the 48 should be struck out of the Freeholders book as usual, in the presence of the parties." Out of these 48 men, 12 were selected by both lawyers to be the jurors.

The results of John Peter Zenger's trial were cause for great celebration. The decision paved the way for journalists who wished to reveal the existence of corruption and deceit in their governments.

On
Trial

When the trial began on August 4, 1735, the courtroom was packed and there were crowds in the street. Just as things were about to get under way, James Alexander appeared. With him was an old man who walked slowly and seemed to be in pain. The gentleman was Andrew Hamilton, an important lawyer from Philadelphia who had traveled with Alexander from Pennsylvania to help Chambers defend John Peter Zenger. Mr. Hamilton began:

> May it please your Honors, I am concerned in this cause on the part of Mr.

Zenger, the defendant. In the common course of proceedings, Mr. Attorney General would be called upon to prove that my client printed and published those newspapers. But I cannot think it proper for me to deny his having published complaints which I think are the right of every freeborn person to make. And therefore I'll save Mr. Attorney General the trouble of examining his witnesses to that point. I do, for my client, confess that he both printed and published the two newspapers quoted in the Information. And I hope in so doing he has committed no crime.

This shocked everyone in the courtroom. Peter's own lawyer had confessed that he had indeed printed criticisms about the government. At this, Attorney General Bradley said the jury was only to decide whether or not Zenger had printed the articles. Once they decided that, it was up to the judge to decide if they were libelous. Knowing that Judge Delancey would of course say they were libelous, and that Peter would then be hanged, Hamilton had another plan—one that would change history.

Since no one was denying that Peter had printed the articles, the witnesses were dismissed. Now the lawyers would argue back and forth on the matter of whether or not what Peter had published was libel. Bradley said that those in the government had to have the respect of the people. Therefore, he reasoned, that anything printed against the governor was libel.

Hamilton objected to that line of reasoning by asking if the people had no right to complain if they were being treated unjustly. He argued that the statements were true, and if they were true, they were not libelous. He said he could call witnesses to testify that what Zenger had printed was true.

Judge Delancey did not like the idea of witnesses. He spoke up and said it did not matter if the statements were true or not, only that they were against the governor. He ordered

Andrew Hamilton led the defense of John Peter Zenger in his trial for libel. His bold argument that it is the right of every free individual to question and reveal the faults of their governments would prove very important in the jury's final decision. This argument paved the way for freedom of the press in America.

Hamilton to stop his arguments. But the old lawyer was bold and not about to give up. He also had earned the respect of many people in the colonies in his long career. He could not easily be silenced. He turned to the jurors and told them that it was up to them to decide, that naturally the court did not want witnesses to testify about what all of New York knew to be true.

Bradley talked about other trials in the law books where printers had been punished and so must this printer. Hamilton quoted from cases where the jury could indeed decide what had happened and the law on how to deal with it. He made an impressive speech:

> The question before the court and you, gentlemen of the jury, is not of small nor private concern. It is not the cause of the poor printer, nor of New York alone, which you are now trying. It may in its consequences affect every freeman in America. It is the best cause. It is the cause of liberty!

The real question being decided was this: were newspapers allowed to let citizens know what their government was doing without being punished?

The trial was ending and Judge Delancey told the jury to find Peter Zenger guilty. The jurors left the courtroom to decide whether Peter was guilty or innocent—and to decide if newspapers could be free to print the truth. Zenger describes the end of the trial: "The jury withdrew, and returned in a small time. Being asked by the clerk whether they were agreed on their **verdict,** and whether John Peter Zenger was guilty of printing and publishing the libels in the information mentioned, they answered by Thomas Hunt, their foreman, 'Not guilty.' Upon which there were three **huzzas** in the hall, which was crowded with people; and the next day I was discharged from my imprisonment." Judge Delancey tried to quiet the room but gave up and walked out. Still, Peter could not be freed because he had to have an order from the judge and Delancey wasn't there. He spent one more night in jail and was released the next day after appearing in court with his lawyer before the judge.

The Popular Party held a celebration that night at the Black Horse Tavern with more than 40 people, and Andrew Hamilton was honored for his defense. The Popular Party's **motto** was on the wall: "LIBERTY and LAW!" The next day, Hamilton left New York and the _Journal_ reported:

> At his departure next day he was saluted with the great guns of several ships in the harbor as a public testimony of his glorious defense he had made in the cause of liberty.

Governor Cosby did not try to silence the press any more. In fact, several months after the trial he became ill. When winter arrived he developed a fever and, in the early spring, he died. Judge Delancey turned out to be much different from the man who had tried the case.

Two years after the trial, he ran for the legislative assembly and was successful. He must have done a lot of thinking during those two years because he ended up being involved in the rights of the people. Before Cosby died, the king's officers in London sent word that ex-Judge Morris had been wrongfully expelled and he was appointed royal governor of New Jersey. Alexander and Morris were allowed to practice law again.

As for Peter, he rested for a couple of weeks, then continued the printing of the City Charter, which had begun before his arrest. With the help of Alexander, he also published all of the legal documents from his case, titled *The Case and Tryal of John Peter Zenger*. It was the most famous book published in America at the time. Peter printed several editions and two were printed in Boston. The trial influenced freedoms in England; five editions were printed in London. Peter continued printing the *Journal*. He became more of a journalist; he printed the facts, even if they caused a stir, but he left out some of the more daring passages. When William Bradford, the older printer of the *Gazette,* could no longer do the public printing for New York, the legislative assembly assigned the job to Peter. Even after all of this, Peter was a poor man.

Eleven years after the trial, Peter died. But Catherine continued printing the *Journal,* which appeared with the statement "Printed by the Widow Catherine Zenger."

John Peter Zenger was born in a struggle to be free and spent his life in **pursuit** of freedom. He fought with a strong weapon—words. And he won. His trial was responsible for first establishing freedom of speech and freedom of the press in America. Lawyers, still to this day, use Zenger's trial as an example when presenting their cases in courtrooms.

Lewis Morris Jr.'s son became Governor Lewis Morris III, a leading statesman. He had fine literary skill and was chosen to write the

Lewis Morris III became a leading states-man in the colonies and wrote the finished version of the Constitution of the United States. He looked back on the trial of Zenger as one of the defining moments in the eventual independence of the United States.

finished version of the Constitution of the United States. It was he who said, "The trial of Zenger was the germ of American freedom."

GLOSSARY

aldermen members of a governing body who represented the different districts

assemblyman someone elected to serve on an assembly, or decision-making group of people

attorney general the lawyer for the government

bail temporary release from jail received by paying money

British from Britain; the same as English

huzzahs shouts that express joy, encouragement, or triumph

indict to accuse formally of an act that is punishable by law

journeyman someone who has finished as an apprentice and is now a worker

jury a group of people chosen to hear evidence in a court case

legislature a law-making body

libel a statement published without just cause

motto a saying or slogan

pound a unit of British money

pursuit search

refugees displaced people

sedition resistance against lawful authority

struck jury chosen jury

verdict a decision made by a jury during trial

CHRONOLOGY

1697 John Peter Zenger is born in western Germany, in an area called Palatinate.

1710 Sails to America with his father, mother, brother, and sister; his father dies on the ship.

1710 Apprenticed to the printer William Bradford for eight years.

1718 Moves to Maryland, sets up printing shop, and marries.

1719 His first child, a son, is born; his wife dies a few months later.

1722 Returns to New York; marries Anna Catharina "Catherine" Maulin on September 11.

1723 Becomes a citizen in New York with the right to vote.

1725 Becomes William Bradford's partner.

1726 Sets up own shop on Smith Street.

1733 *New York Weekly Journal* is started.

1734 Arrested and jailed on November 17; Catherine Zenger manages the *Journal* while Peter is in jail.

1735 Tried on August 4; jury reaches a verdict of not guilty; Zenger is freed from jail on August 5.

1736 Publishes *The Case and Tryal of John Peter Zenger.*

1746 Dies on July 28.

COLONIAL TIME LINE

1607 Jamestown, Virginia, is settled by the English.

1620 Pilgrims on the *Mayflower* land at Plymouth, Massachusetts.

1623 The Dutch settle New Netherlands, the colony that later becomes New York.

1630 Massachusetts Bay Colony is started.

1634 Maryland is settled as a Roman Catholic colony. Later Maryland becomes a safe place for people with different religious beliefs.

1636 Roger Williams is thrown out of the Massachusetts Bay Colony. He settles Rhode Island, the first colony to give people freedom of religion.

1682 William Penn forms the colony of Pennsylvania.

1688 Pennsylvania Quakers make the first formal protest against slavery.

1692 Trials for witchcraft are held in Salem, Massachusetts.

1712 Slaves revolt in New York. Twenty-one blacks are killed as punishment.

1720 Major smallpox outbreak occurs in Boston. Cotton Mather and some doctors try a new treatment. Many people think the new treatment shouldn't be used.

1754 French and Indian War begins. It ends nine years later.

1761 Benjamin Banneker builds a wooden clock that keeps precise time.

1765 Britain passes the Stamp Act. Violent protests break out in the colonies. The Stamp Act is ended the next year.

1775 The battles of Lexington and Concord begin the American Revolution.

1776 Declaration of Independence is signed.

FURTHER READING

Carlson, Laurie M. *Colonial Kids: An Activity Guide to Life in the New World*. Chicago: Chicago Review Press, 1997.

Evans, J. Edwards. *Freedom of the Press*. Minneapolis, MN: Lerner Publications, 1990.

Kalman, Bobbie. *Colonial Life*. New York: Crabtree Publishers, 1992.

King, David C. *Colonial Days: Discover the Past with Fun Projects, Games, Activities, and Recipes*. New York: John Wiley, 1997.

——. *The Right to Speak Out*. Brookfield, CT: Millbrook Press, 1997.

Smith, C. Carter, ed. *Daily Life: A Sourcebook on Colonial America*. Brookfield, CT: Millbrook Press, 1991.

Warner, John F. *Colonial American Home Life*. Danbury, CT: Franklin Watts, 1993.

INDEX

INDEX

PICTURE CREDITS

ABOUT THE AUTHOR

KAREN T. WESTERMANN is a writer and editor in vocational education. She is also a freelance writer of adult fiction and has had poetry, a children's book, and feature articles published. She has a degree in English and lives in rural Virginia with her family, three dogs, and three cats.

Senior Consulting Editor **ARTHUR M. SCHLESINGER, JR.** is the leading American historian of our time. He won the Pulitzer Prize for his book *The Age of Jackson* (1945) and again for *A Thousand Days* (1965). This chronicle of the Kennedy Administration also won a National Book Award. He has written many other books including a multi-volume series, *The Age of Roosevelt*. Professor Schlesinger is the Albert Schweitzer Professor of the Humanities at the City University of New York, and has been involved in several other Chelsea House projects, including the REVOLUTIONARY WAR LEADERS biographies on the most prominent figures of early American history.